HEALTH, WEALTH, & BALANCE

THROUGH FENG SHUI

by

Elaine Jay Finster

ACKNOWLEDGMENTS

I wish to thank Dean and Phyllis Stonier of Thornton, Colorado for their efforts to educate the seekers of this world. They started the summer Global Sciences program in Denver, Colorado in 1983. The Stoniers bring interesting and controversial speakers and researchers to broaden the mind and allow the participants to reëvaluate their concepts, principles and lifestyles. This is where I first was introduced to Feng Shui.

I wish to thank the following people:

Susan Blackburn final proofreader
Dhyane Markley cover design and illustrations
Sue Trumpfeller who shared her video's
Iris Kinney shared stories and testimonials
Beth Murphy layout and design of the book
Stanley Bytnar for proofreading
Ronald Blackburn computer layout and graphics

Master Lin Yun, for his transcendental wisdom.

COPYRIGHT © 1991-1999 by Elaine Jay Finster. All rights reserved.

No part of this publication may be reproduced or transmitted in any form, including electrical, mechanical, photocopy, or any other means of retrieval. Short passages may be used for review in magazines and newspapers.

Published in the United States by New Age Concepts, P.O. Box 93, Bailey, CO 80421-0093, phone (303) 838-8446, fax (303) 838-2282

First edition , August 1991
Second edition , February 19, 1996
Revised third edition , March 1999, Year of the Rabbit

ISBN 1-886844-11-9

THE YEAR OF TIBET

The Tibetan Royal Year of 2118
March 10, 1991 - March, 1992

This book is dedicated to the global effort to save
Tibet before its culture and people disappear.

Tibet was overtaken by communist Chinese in 1950. Over
forty years of silent massacre has befallen these people.

* Over 1/6 of its people died at the hands of invaders.
* All religious practices are outlawed.
* More then 6,000 temples and historic sites are looted.
* Virgin forests have been cut and sold by the enemy.
* Religious jewels and art have been looted or destroyed.
* His Holiness the Dalai Lama fled for his life.

A donation from each book will be used to assist Tibet House.

For further information on this project contact:
Tibet House, 241 E. 32 St. New York, NY. 10016, 212-213-5592

The logo is used with permission of Anne Souza, Director.

TABLE OF CONTENTS

ACKNOWLEDGMENTS	ii
THE YEAR OF TIBET	iii
PREFACE	v
INTRODUCTION	vii
CHAPTER ONE	1
OVERVIEW	1
CHAPTER TWO	3
SITTING AT THE MASTER'S FEET	3
CHAPTER THREE	12
ABSOLUTE INGREDIENTS	12
CHAPTER FOUR	16
EIGHT ASPECTS OF LIFE	16
TRIGRAM CHART	18
CHAPTER FIVE	19
NINE CURES	19
CHAPTER SIX	23
LOVE & MARRIAGE	23
CHAPTER SEVEN	27
HOME AND HEALTH	27
CHAPTER EIGHT	31
BUSINESS	31
CHAPTER NINE	34
WEALTH & PROSPERITY	34
CHAPTER TEN	37
CHINESE ZODIAC	37
CHAPTER ELEVEN	39
TESTIMONIALS	39
GLOSSARY	43
FENG SHUI ITEMS	44
NEW ITEMS	45
ESSENTIAL OILS	46
BIOGRAPHY	47

PREFACE

There are many pieces to the great puzzle of life. As I traveled my personal road joining the pieces of the puzzle together, I came across what I believe to be the most important segment.

I attended a series of New Thought lectures in the summer of 1988. One speaker presented ancient secrets of the Chinese. My interest peaked immediately. I knew at that moment I needed to research this obscure subject called Feng Shui (pronounced fong schway). These words literally mean "wind and water" and it has been successfully practiced over 3000 years in China and neighboring countries including Japan, Tibet, and India.

Professor Thomas Lin Yun was responsible for bringing this ancient art of placement to our western shores. In 1990 I had an opportunity to meet some of Master Lin's students and learn more about this fascinating subject. One student was so kind she sent me video tapes dubbed in English so I could continue my education. My studies included every available book in English on Feng Shui as well as attending lectures. The library helped me locate recent articles in national publications. I exchanged knowledge with other Feng Shui students and consultants. I spent time with the Vietnamese shopkeepers in my city who were most anxious to share and teach me about Buddha and various good luck charms to keep negative ch'i away. In my travels throughout the United States, I found that many people knew something about this philosophy. With all these experiences I was able to weave the parts into a glittering and compelling tapestry.

In the fall of 1990 I presented my first public lecture on Feng Shui, THE ART OF PLACEMENT. Over 90 people attended the lecture in Denver, Colorado. One lady engaged me to use my tools and investigate why her house was not selling. I suggested making some changes. A short while later the house sold, allowing her to avoid filing bankruptcy.

At that moment I knew I was beginning a journey that had no end.

With winter easing into spring I meditated on my decision that in the fall I would go to Berkeley, California and personally study with the world famous Feng Shui master. I called the Yun Lin Temple to inquire when classes started and was told that Master Lin would be teaching an intensive workshop outside of New York City in late June. I immediately called the phone number given and made arrangements. Nothing mattered; time stood still for me; I was accepted into the inner circle as one of Master Lin's students. My dream became a reality. I was to learn the Feng Shui secrets and transcendental cures practiced by Black Hat Sect Buddhists.

During the first few days of the workshop my intent was to learn as many secrets as I could. I found my greatest gift was to meditate using the Buddhist ancient discipline. This pure form of energy cleared my mind and gave me strength while it dissolved stress and worry. I now know how to open my heart center and be one with the divine cosmic energy. I will share this particular meditation with my readers.

As a student of Master Lin, I was taught how to properly recite and ritually practice the "Great Sunshine Buddha" meditation. After 27 days of faithful practice, I noticed that I was more content with myself and a feeling of balance and harmony existed deep within. I also noticed that I had to change my eating habits. I found I couldn't eat certain foods. This was evident after drinking a can of Pepsi™. I had trouble digesting the liquid, something that had never happened before. Although I eat very little red meat or poultry, I now get either indigestion or diarrhea about one hour after the meal. A few sips of wine will make me dizzy, followed by an intense headache.

My interpretation of these changes is that more light has entered my body and my personal awareness is heightened. Therefore, foods in the lower food chain are being rejected. Because of these changes when I practice Feng Shui, I am able to be more sensitive to the subject at hand.

I have talked to several people who refer to themselves as Feng Shui Consultants. Although they understand the basics of this complex subject, they are not giving the 120% that Master Lin talks about that is needed to rectify a situation. This book will be of help to add the missing ingredients.

When one sits and studies under the watchful eye of the master, there is an unfurling of wisdom that enriches the student. I have now dedicated my life work to the study and practice of Feng Shui principles. I wish to assist others who are seeking a new solution to an old problem.

INTRODUCTION

For centuries China has been a mystery to the world. One of the most obvious mysteries was the Great Wall of China. We have only lately learned in the West that the great wall was built with Feng Shui principles. The architects and geomancers did not want to cut the veins of the dragon. The Chinese believe the earth emanates energy and if that energy were to be weakened or interfered with it could be devastating to the residents. They seek to maintain harmony with the forces of nature.

The practice of Feng Shui began over 3000 years ago to locate the ideal grave site. As time went on farmers began to be advised by Buddhist priests who were the first Feng Shui experts where and when to plant crops and the most ideal location for the family abode. Villages, towns, and later cities were built with the Feng Shui principles, most of which still exist today.

In 1972, a Buddhist priest and scholar graced our shore and began implementing and teaching the oral tradition of these mystical arts. Professor Thomas Lin Yun began his studies of the Black Hat Tibetan Tantric Sect of Buddhism (TTB) at the age of six. He is a native of China where he spent many years studying Buddhism and the mystical arts which included Feng Shui.

As a student of Master Lin, I will attempt to bring understanding of this complicated subject to the beginner and intermediate student alike. There are several transcendental solutions to situations that have not appeared in print before. Master Lin has encouraged his students to share some of the ancient guarded knowledge with those who sincerely seek answers.

There are several books on the subject of Feng Shui and they all seem to contradict each other, confusing the reader. Each author has studied under a different Buddhist Sect. There are five recognized schools of thought and practice. These are the Nyagnopa (red hat), Geluypa (yellow hat), Kayupa (white hat), Sakyapa (mixed hat), and Bon (black hat). The first four are the more traditional schools. Each writer focuses on their particular discipline. This book will focus on the Black Hat sect teachings. The TTB uses both orthodox and unorthodox methodologies to make determinations and carry out solutions.

This book is designed so that the reader can locate a problem and carry out the solution or cure. The areas that will be addressed are as follows: Home - most and least desirous shapes. How to rectify a problem area for the least expense and the most positive results. Do's and don'ts in office arrangements. Understanding the ba-gua, an octagon shape, also referred to as the eight trigrams, and the power of each direction.

There are various shapes, numbers, colors and cures that will influence one's decisions. Utilizing the various tools allows the user to make strong, clear choices.

Finally, many people struggle with relationships both personal and work related. Among the many reasons for this is the placement of the master bedroom, the floor plan of the house or astrologically the parties involved are of opposing zodiac years.

You will learn to fine tune yourself and your surroundings through the ancient mysteries of Feng Shui. The ultimate goal is to be in balance with your personal universe. The Chinese always place south on the top.

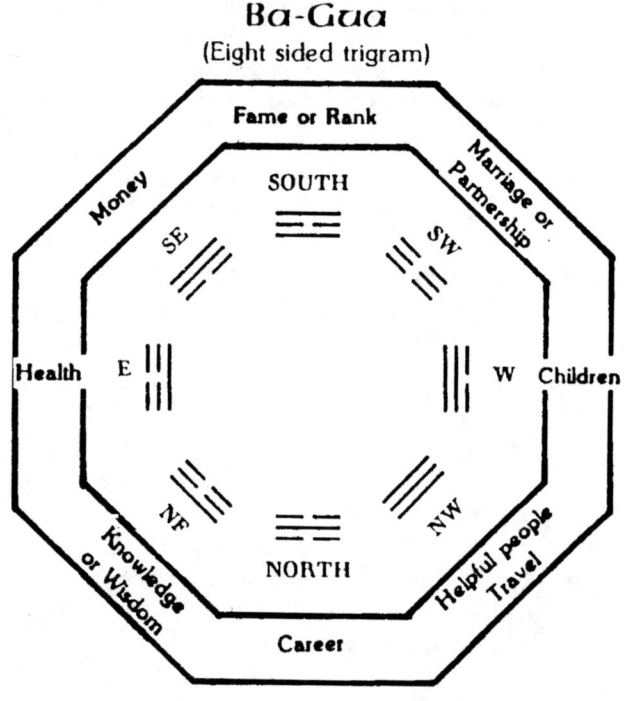

CHAPTER ONE
OVERVIEW

The Orient has always had a deep mysterious side to it. In the recent past, China has shared her secrets to quiet the mind and strengthen the body through Martial Arts. Our next gift was the use of Acupuncture, which in now practiced by many western doctors. Now, after many centuries, we have been given the gift of adjusting our living and working space to bring health, wealth, and balance into our daily lives. Feng Shui is the principle of humanity in balance with its surroundings.

Some of these deeply guarded secrets were first brought to the West by a European over a century ago. Ernest J. Eitel, a missionary, who took a post in China, had learned first hand about the mystical arts practiced by the Chinese populace. In 1873, he published the first book on Feng Shui, "The Science of Sacred Landscape". Europeans found the subject matter interesting but had a hard time understanding the concepts. This was caused in part by Eitel's Christian doctrine which discounted many beliefs and practices as old wives' tales.

It was over a century before the subject would be in print again. Sarah Rossbach, under the guidance of Master Lin Yun, wrote "Feng Shui: The Chinese Art of Placement" in 1983. Her second book "Interior Design with Feng Shui" followed in 1986. These were unique for two reasons. The books were written by a non-Asian woman. Prior to this time Feng Shui had been passed down in the oral tradition from father to son.

Master Lin resides in Berkeley, California where he teaches, lectures, and consults for large corporations and private individuals. In 1986, he established the first temple of the Black Hat sect Tibetan Tantric Buddhism in North America.

The traditional Feng Shui schools use absolute directions (north, south, east, west) to determine their recommendations. The placement of the Ba-Gua (or the eight avenues of life) is determined by using a compass also known as a luopan. Tangible factors, which include objective shapes, are strongly emphasized.

Black Hat is unorthodox in its approach. Directions are arrived at by determining the "Mouth of Ch'i," which is the front door. It is also called the three north door theory. The front door, if it is directly in the center, is considered north, if it is to the far left of the building it is northeast, to the far right, northwest. It does not matter how often you enter through this door or if you never use it, the front door is the front door.

Each room can be assessed separately by its placement to the entry door (Mouth of Ch'i) of that room. More often than not the Feng Shui expert will superimpose the Ba-Gua over the whole first floor to make direction assessments. This means you take all the rooms on the first floor and section out the eight directions using the front door as your "mouth of ch'i". The opposite end of the house is the (center) south direction. Both methods are acceptable. The Black Hat school of thought states that nothing is absolute or stationary. This is why they do not use a compass. Instead, the front door is the compass which dictates north (if it is in the center). It uses both tangible factors as well as intangible concepts to make assessments. The key to this methodology is in reinforcing the "Three Secrets." If the three secrets are not used the ch'i change will not be as effective.

Nine basic cures are at one's disposal to readjust the energies. These include sound, color, bamboo flutes or beaded curtains, living objects, heavy objects, mobiles, bright lights, firecrackers, and electrically powered objects. The most favored are mirrors, crystals, and aquariums.

The ba-gua is an eight sided pattern or octagon. Each gua represents a direction of life. These include prosperity, children or creativity, knowledge, fame/rank, family, career, helpful people/travel, and marriage or relationships. By knowing the exact direction of each gua, adjustments can be enhanced or readjusted to bring forth a transcendental cure.

The Black Hat school focuses on the bed in the master bedroom and the location of the bedroom. Ideally it should be behind the center line of the house toward the rear. If the bed is not in a favorable placement it can be a key factor for lack of promotion at work, stress, being accident prone, insomnia, and possible chronic illness.

Four mystical animals represent cardinal directions. They are revered as the earth protection spirits. The most ideal are the azure dragon, east and the white tiger, west. They are the yin and yang of structural placement. The red bird phoenix is south, and the black tortoise represents north. Many homes and businesses will have the animal protectors in their specific direction to ensure health and good luck. The dragon brings the sun up from the east and keeps evil or harmful spirits away. At most Chinese celebrations, the dragon represents protection. It weaves itself along the street and chases away any bad luck and negative spirits.

CHAPTER TWO
SITTING AT THE MASTER'S FEET

As I sat in the OMEGA Institute in upstate New York on a cool June day, I had high expectations of what was to be presented in the weeklong class. I arrived early to get a front row seat. At exactly 9 a.m. a portly, cheerful Chinese man entered with his entourage of young Chinese followers and interpreters.

We were formally introduced to Master Lin as Professor Lin Yun, Grand Master of Tantric Buddhism Black Hat School. He was casually dressed in a polo shirt, slacks, and comfortable sandals. We quickly realized that the master spoke no English. Patricia Shia, a wonderful young Chinese woman, did an excellent job as his main interpreter. Cecelia Wong had the difficult task of selecting the appropriate overhead slides. Robert Chiu, a student at Stanford University, videotaped the workshop for the temple's private files.

Master Lin started by saying "Feng Shui is a means to deflect ill fortune and attract good luck."

That first morning of class we learned that the scenery one sees on the way to work will affect the person's outlook toward life. If one sees dark, dry, barren land he will feel sad and not fulfill his potential. On the other hand, if there is a lot of greenery and flowers this person will be happy and be full of life when he arrives at work. Greenery always brings happiness and joy.

If one lives near a funeral home or cemetery it lowers one's mood. I mentioned this to a relative who had lived two blocks from four large cemeteries. She reflected back to when she lived there and remembered feeling sad almost daily. After she moved her mood was better and her health improved.

We were taught to pick the most appropriate place to live and work through Feng Shui methods. There are external factors to examine, i.e., such as how close the road is to the house, how close telephone poles or transformers are located to the house (they can cause strange diseases and frequent quarreling), whether there is a pointed roof directed at the house, or the proximity to churches or temples (which can cause sadness).

We learned internal factors included potential bed position, stove placement relative to the door, existence of overhead beams, tall bookshelves, and various types of staircases.

The next evaluation was to determine the reasons for the sale of a property. These could be good, such as job promotion, moving from a small house to a larger one, and marriage; or negative such as injury, death, bankruptcy, legal problems, divorce, lost job or demotion, or moving to a smaller house.

When inspecting property, look for the positive signs such as the dragon points, which are bright splashes of green growth that will attract the eye. Bad indications are a dead bird near the doorway, bare or yellow spots in the lawn, light bulbs going out or exploding within the first three days of installation, stuck and/or broken screens or doors. Squawking birds such as magpies, crows, or vultures are not good signs, but melodic birds and hummingbirds are.

One slogan Master Lin set in our minds was, "Four ounces of adjustment is worth 1,000 pounds of cure." He, of course, was referring to the nine cures used in Feng Shui treatments.

Our afternoon lesson covered the importance of ch'i. Ch'i is the real you. He went on to say our body is only a empty shell, ch'i makes us move, rest, think, and speak. Ch'i is either in the static state (stationary) or the dynamic state (state of movement). There are some people whose ch'i is stuck. They talk and talk but never think about what they are saying, the ch'i bypasses the brain. Other individuals have something to say but the ch'i is stuck in the throat, they are good listeners but need the opportunity to share their thoughts. The porcupine ch'i is one who hurts others either physically or with insults. The most desirable ch'i is the smooth balance type. This person thinks before speaking and acts with loving, up-lifting intentions. There are other ch'i types which include introverted, hot & cold, day-dreamer, distracted, and suicidal ch'i. He spent some time on this type of individual and encouraged us to work with the suicidal ch'i because they are doing great harm to themselves. These individuals will have drooped shoulders or are bent over. They also sigh frequently and live a hermetic life with anti-social behavior. They often think others want to hurt them. Master Lin reminded us that the greatest gift in life is to assist a life.

He then directed us in how to do the <u>Sunshine Buddha Exercise</u> and recite the six true words. It's essential to use mantras for 27 consecutive days to balance and blend one's ch'i to a more ideal state.

He also stated the Black Hat sect does not know or recognize the words "no" or "can't." This came up when a class participant asked if there are any secrets the Black Hat sect uses for fertility. The master began by explaining his interpretation of Ling particles. These particles are often referred to as atoms in the western community. When the female wishes to become pregnant he advised that she not dust under the bed or clean the bedroom. This is because the ling particles that enter a woman upon conception are on, under, or near the bed. There is a special meditation one can use during sexual union to increase the chances of pregnancy. Our interpreter, Patricia, explained it is not easy to concentrate on the meditation during that time. Her eyes got large as she spoke and we all laughed with empathy.

We were also instructed that during pregnancy it is bad luck to move to a new residence because the unborn child will be restless or not have a strong direction as he or she grows up. One should rest as much as possible, and not bother oneself by picking up heavy things or moving furniture.

The second day I joined other students for Ta'i Ch'i at 6:00 a.m. so I could flex my body as well as my mind. We stood in front of a small lake and watched the sun rise as we quietly went through our Ta'i Ch'i paces.

After breakfast I ran up the hill to the classroom, ready to learn more of the age-old secrets such as "Sprinkling the Rice" and "The Cut Flower Ritual" and how to perform them. The first secret was "Sealing the Door." If there had been a robbery, a recent death, or a chain of back luck, then the sealing of the door was the mystical cure to dispense the negative energy. This secret is explained in Chapter Three.

Bed positioning is the most important aspect of Feng Shui. If the bed is in direct line of the doorway, many ill effects will befall the person. These can be anything from being accident prone to being unsuccessful at work. The Chinese refer to this as the coffin bed. When a person died in their bed the corpse was always carried out feet first through the doorway. If there is no other possible way to change the bed position then the one solution would be to hang a faceted crystal between the foot of the bed and the doorway. This will deflect the fast running ch'i in the room.

The most ideal bed placement is kitty-corner from the door. If this is not possible, position a mirror so you can get a clear view of the door entrance. It is not a good idea to place a bed against a wall (that is to say the headboard and one whole side) since it interferes with the circulation of ch'i. If you do not have an alternative, then hang a wind chime above the bed. The wind chime clears the mind and adjusts the personal ch'i.

The third day was full of new and more complicated techniques. The master demonstrated the touching of the 27 heavy objects which include: sofa, desk, stove, bed, etc. We were told touching the objects will adjust irregular ch'i in a house or apartment. It is wise to do this ch'i adjustment once a year.

A much simpler technique was to adjust personal body ch'i using specific areas (gua's) in the bedroom. "Why the bedroom" a student asked? And we were told that the bedroom is where we spend one third of our lives sleeping and resting; this is where the body comes to heal. It is important to note that <u>the bed's direction is different than that of the bedroom</u>. The bed is its own entity, the head of the bed is always considered south, feet north, right side is east. The bedroom is determined by the door position, the door of any room (Mouth of Ch'i) is always north if in the center, northwest to the far right, and northeast to the far left. This is referred to as the moving trigram. When we assess the body, south is always at the top of head or the eye area. Mouth and teeth are west, hip is southeast, foot is north. If there is some difficulty or discomfort in a particular body area then adjust the bedroom direction related to that specific part or parts with one of the following: a red cloth, hanging crystal ball on a 9-inch (or increments of nine) red-silk string, mirror or wind chime to correct the difficulty (red is life force or energy). Of course, he stated, "I am not a doctor and if medical attention is required, do that first." One story was told of a man who had weak ankles. He noted that the north direction of his bedroom had a pile of books and papers that were just thrown there. After he neatly rearranged the pile and placed them on a bookshelf, his ankles began to strengthen. Another success story was related about a lady who had eye problems and after adjusting the south direction in her bedroom, her sight improved considerably. There is a direct relationship between good vision through windows and eye problems. The first step to better vision is to correct damaged or cracked windows or windshields. Follow the adjustment with the "three secrets" to complete and activate the adjustment.

As we learned placement in homes and shapes of houses, several students brought to the attention of Master Lin that New Yorkers usually lived in apartment buildings. Would he please describe the placement of the ba-gua and whether the total building is a factor or not? He answered the question starting with a court yard. "This," he said, "will have an affect on the residence as does the placement of the entry door." One's individual apartment will have the most influence on the resident but never discount the placement of the first two entries (building and courtyard).

We were instructed in how to use the moving-in ritual. This can be performed on either a home or business. Tie or wrap a nine-inch red ribbon around a white vase, place a bamboo flute that also has a red ribbon or tassel on it in the vase. Walk around the building carrying the vase and flute, find an auspicious spot to set it for a period of nine days. If this is not feasible, place the vase in an eye catching position in the room and the flute on the wall with the mouthpiece downward. Complete the ceremony with the "three secrets." The three secrets are further explained in Chapter Three. This will bring positive new beginnings into your new surroundings.

Selecting a plot of land can make all the difference between success and struggle. It is best to have a square, round, or rectangular lot. If the plot is in the shape of an animal, lady, or clam that is also desirable. Never build on top of a mountain, however, just below the top of the mountain on a flat shelf of land is usually all right. Don't have your front door facing the mountain because it will block career success.

If the land is clam-shaped, place the house near the middle where the clam muscle would be to add strength to the residents. The most desirous plot of land is two hills with a valley or plateau between. This is referred to as "two dragons and a pearl." The house should be in the pearl position in the valley. This house is assured success and residents are advised to go into banking or business.

If a lot is odd-shaped, such as oblong with a short or cut-off edge, one can plant bamboo, use bamboo stakes, or install a flood light on a pole to balance the imperfection. You ideally want a squared off corner.

The first room one enters affects how one reacts to life. For instance, if you enter the house and the first thing you see is food or the stove which prepares the food you will have a tendency to overeat and frequently have problems with digestion or digestive diseases i.e.: ulcers, obesity, or heartburn. I have this arrangement in my house. I asked Master Lin if anything can be done to change this negative problem. He answered, "Place an item such as a book case in a location that your eye will focus on when entering the house." When I arrived home after the class I did just that. I placed a book case on a far wall so that when I enter my house I now always look at the bookcase first and think of knowledge and study rather than thinking I am hungry. This has made a difference in my eating habits. If the bathroom is first noticed upon entering, subconsciously that person will need to go to the bathroom as soon as they open the door. A living room makes people relaxed and think, they like to write letters or read books, if the T.V. is in sight upon entering the residents will click on the T.V. Bedrooms bring out laziness, these people are frequently tired and often do work in bed. A den or study brings new information and increases career success for adults and better study habits for children. A game room makes children more adventurous and adults tend to engage in more risky business; this could be both good and bad.

If, when entering the house, the first thing you see is a wall, you can get a disease in your midline, back pain, or have slumped shoulders. This will affect your mood and ambition. It has a direct relationship to career success. One often feels blocked. To correct this situation, place a mirror at eye level, but tall enough so that the adults have a full head view. If the tallest resident's head is cut off by the mirror this individual can suffer from headaches as well as not being clear with career or job. A colorful arrangement of flowers can be used in place of the mirror.

A fairly common situation that occurs in American homes is that the residents see a wall with one eye and a long view with the other eye. This is referred to as the "split eye." It can cause a variety of difficulties. To begin with, the optic nerve will be unbalanced, which in turn causes insomnia, arguing with one's spouse, eye problems, and eventually mental breakdown. The Black Hat Feng Shui transcendental solution is to hang a large mirror on the entry wall and also suspend a faceted crystal or brass wind chimes where the long view of the house begins. A second correction is to enter the house from another door that does not pose this problem. If not corrected, usually divorce will result along with problems at work and/or loss of employment.

The placement of the central staircase leading to the first landing has a direct relationship with the conduct of employees. If there is a rest room at top of the stairs, the workers engage in chatter and socializing. They lose their concentration. It will take up to 20 minutes to settle down to the day's work. If at the first landing there is a library, these people, on the other hand, will be studious and bring fresh, new ideas to work. They also start work immediately.

The kitchen is the room of wealth. Place a mirror or tinfoil behind the burners of the stove to double the reflection of four burners into eight. Since the stove is where food is prepared, it is important to rotate your burners so that you use all of them otherwise stagnation occurs. We were advised to eat the best of foods because it nourishes our ch'i. Less expensive or junk food will lower ch'i. A fruit basket or dish should ideally sit on a round or octagon shaped mirror so that it reflects the fruit and doubles the count. Food to the Chinese is synonymous with prosperity.

If the kitchen is located in the south east direction according to the moving trigram associated with the front door being north, this house will always provide financial security to the occupants.

I asked if a person has a ba-gua pattern in their carpet or floor covering, will that insure good luck to the residence? I was a little surprised when he answered, "No." According to Black Hat Feng Shui unless you perform the "Three Secrets" which is a mantra, visualization, and a particular body mudra (hand gesture) then the ba-gua pattern is only an attractive design without a purpose.

On Thursday, our lesson consisted of more advanced techniques which included the ch'i transfusion. Several students requested Master Lin give them a transfusion. The healing ch'i being sent is part of the yellow sun of Buddha. When the transfusion is given the ch'i leaves Master Lin's body and goes to the Buddha to collect the ch'i... then comes back filled with the Buddha's ch'i into his body. The ch'i energy is passed through the fingers as tens of thousands of light rays to the recipient. I noticed each recipient gave Master Lin a red envelope in exchange.

The red envelope is a means of payment to the consultant or practitioner. The ancient tradition is still carried on today. If one adjustment has been performed, then one red envelope is exchanged. If multiple adjustments have been done then nine red envelopes are given. The reason for the exchange is to protect the consultant because they divulged or performed ancient secrets. That night, the Feng Shui practitioner sleeps with the red envelopes under his pillow to seal the exchange.

Our last day of class Master Lin briefly explained the Chinese zodiac system. This will get covered briefly in Chapter 10. Chinese use the year rather than the western method of the month to determine compatibility between business partners or marriage partners.

Compatible Matches

snake-monkey
dog-rabbit
dragon-cock

sheep-horse
pig-tiger
rat-ox

Incompatible Matches

dragon-dog
snake-pig
horse-rat
sheep-ox
monkey-tiger
cock-rabbit

dragon-rabbit
snake-tiger
horse-ox
sheep-rat
monkey-pig
cock-dog

    The Chinese Zodiac works in increments of 30 degrees, if your signs are 120 degrees apart that is good; if your signs are 90 or 180 degrees apart that is bad or incompatible. (The exceptions for the 90 degrees are snake-monkey and pig-tiger.) This gave me new insight as to why some past relationships and partnerships were short in duration. Specific years and character qualities will be covered further in Chapter 10, "Chinese Zodiac."

    To enhance your life path and remove some of the obstacles, use the astrological formula which includes sign, compatible sign, and time of day. Note the best times for you to do business, buy a lottery ticket, have surgical procedures performed, or any other strategic plans that you need time involved to carry out plans more efficiently. For example, the dragon is 7-9 a.m., compatible sign is cock 5-7 p.m. and ox 1-3 a.m. The less compatible signs are dog 7-9 p.m. and rabbit 5-7 a.m. Time is determined by the time zone you are in and time standard currently being used.

    Eight of the twelve signs also represent a special function:

ox = marriage
dragon = helpful people
sheep = knowledge
pig = wealth

tiger
snake
monkey
dog

rabbit = children
horse = career
cock = family
rat = fame

    By spending some time with the Chinese astrology system, an individual can calculate their path of destiny closer to their advantage and bypass some of life's pitfalls. Look in Chapter 10 for your most opportune time slots within your personal zodiac. The most auspicious days are the first, fifteenth and always the ninth because nine is the number of completion and strength. The fifth is also good because it means movement. We are not saying there are bad days, just that these shine over the other days.

All of us were both happy and sad when our workshop was over at the end of the week. We felt saturated with the great wisdom and new secret tools to perform our transcendental cures. We also felt sad because our master who had gently taken us under his wing of guidance and trust would no longer be a handshake away. Although I have been an avid student and practitioner in Feng Shui the past three years, I still had learned much. Master Lin reminded us to do the heart-mind mantra to calm our mind and tap into the great Buddiac wisdom of which he is a part, so that we could be mentally on the same plane of Cosmic Intelligence.

The chart below describes the ideal time to correct or enhance situations. For instance, one o'clock (AM or PM) is the most opportune time to select for strengthening marriage issues or relationships. The oxen represents marriage. An oxen should ideally be placed in the Southwest corner (the marriage corner).

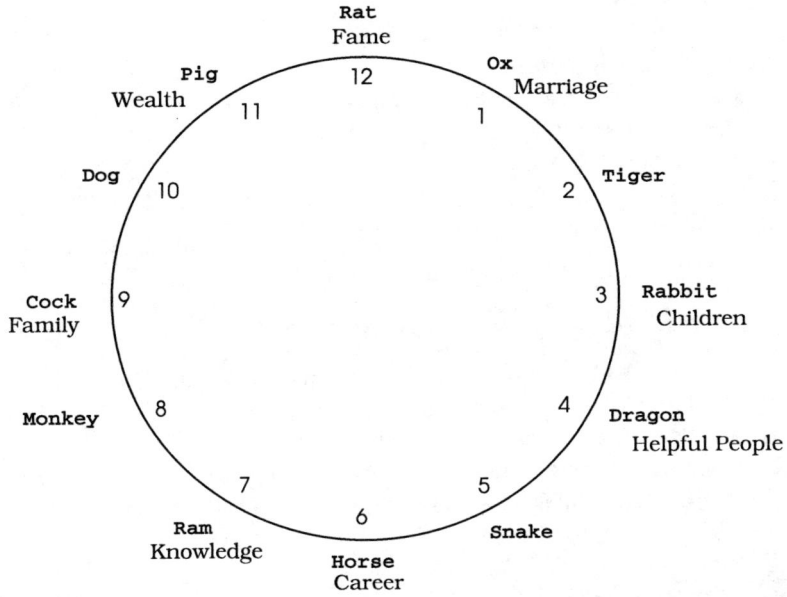

CHAPTER THREE
ABSOLUTE INGREDIENTS

The most important technique when adjusting Feng Shui is always to reinforce the adjustments with "THE THREE SECRETS". This can be thought of as adding glue to the project at hand to give it a more secure foundation. The mystical ingredients are the body, mind, and speech. This is what assures the 120 percent success rate that Master Lin professes. He explains the high percentage rate as twenty percent from the mundane solution and 100 percent from the transcendental solution or cure, which are the Black Hat teachings.

A mundane solution would be to encourage a person to work harder for more money, or take a part time job on weekends in addition to the primary job. This will, of course, bring more money, but there is no time free for family and friends. The Black Hat sect Buddhist would use a transcendental solution that will bring more money with less effort.

Some examples of transcendental cures are placing nine small stones in a plant, wearing a non-metallic ring such as jade or Hematite on the middle finger, or placing a piggy bank under the bed for 27 or 99 days.

First decide what you want the final outcome to be. If you want more money, how best would you obtain it? Would a pay raise help? If self employed, do you need new products or accounts? Perhaps a better job is the best solution. Once the ideal solution is chosen select from the reinforcements below.

The three secret reinforcements are the cement mentioned above. There are the body mudras, secret speech/mantras (chants) and visualization always using multiples of nine.

The Three Secrets

The body mudra is the various hand positions. You will choose one best suited for the solution. The ousting mudra is flicking bad or negative situations, people, or circumstances away from you. This is done by extending the index and the pinky fingers forward. With the two middle fingers and thumb make a motion as if you were flicking away something.

The ousting hand mudra is used more frequently than some of the others. It is recommended that males use the left hand and females use the right hand when performing this mudra.

The heart and mind calming gesture is as follows: Gently cup your right hand palm up, then place your left hand on top, gently touching the thumbs together. Hold your hands either at chest level or near the waist. This hand gesture can be used to bring peace and clarity to the individual and or the situation.

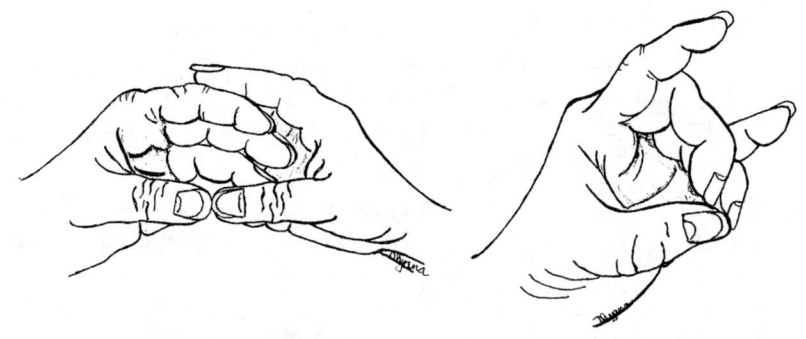

Heart Mind Mudra   **Ousting Mudra**

Another favorite mudra is the "Great Sunshine Buddha Meditation," which is used to bring better health or renewal of energy. Stand with your feet facing forward 18 inches apart, put your hands above your head with palms up toward the real or imagined sun, keeping the elbows bent a little. See drawing on next page. Visualize the sun's rays entering your body through the center of your palms and forehead. Feel the rays circulating down through your base chakra and up, exiting your palms. Next visualize the energy entering the palms, passing through the body and exiting from the bottom of your feet. Lower your hands if tired. Repeat the pose, this time see the sun's rays again entering your palms, pacing through the body to the feet and returning upward. As the energy is raising, see it coiling slowly throughout the body, taking with it all the pain and toxic cells from the sick parts of the body. It will exit through your palms and head "the three entry points." Often, you will feel an inflated beam of energy or light about the ears to the crown of the head.

The speech secret or mantra involves chanting or saying words. The most important are the six true words. Recite **"Om Ma Ne Pad Me Hum"** nine times for a simple ch'i adjustment. For the Buddha exercise, recite the words 27 times three times a day, equaling a total of 81 times. It's important to recite your chants upon waking, mid-day, and at bedtime. Mentally think your special intent while chanting the six true words. A complete cycle is daily for 27 or 99 days. If you are making a transcendental correction to recycle the energy or dispel bad ch'i, it is not necessary to say the six true words 81 times. Recite the six true words just 9 times. The six true words translate to **"The jewel in the center of the heart beats in the center of the Universe."**

The heart and mind calming mantra to adjust personal ch'i is best recited at bedtime in place of taking a sleeping pill. Recite **"Gah tee, Gah tee, Bora gah tee, Boro sun gah tee, Bodhi, So po he."** Say this three times. Relaxation and sleep will soon follow.

The mind secret uses visualization. Ideally say your chants and use the body mudras while visualizing the outcome of the solution. For example, if you place nine stones in a green plant you can visualize more money pouring into the household, or increased business. It is not essential to see and do all these simultaneously. You can first do the body mudra and speech mantra and directly after visualize your desire, or outcome.

If you have had bad luck, a recent robbery, or there has been a death at your home, "Sealing the Door" cure is called for. This technique should also be used when moving into a new home or office or if your home is next to or in view of a church. This transcendental cure should be carried out by the head of the household.

In a cup or bowl put one teaspoon of Realgar (arsenic sulfide). Add alcohol rum or whiskey to this from unopened bottle, one drop of liquor for every year of the head of the family's age plus one. Or total up the years of all the members of the household plus one extra drop per person. Stir with middle finger, nine times. Use the left hand for a man, and the right for a women.

Dot the main entry door starting at the top center. Second, dot the door at eye level above the doorknob. The third drop goes by the doorknob and the last one approximately nine inches above the floor.

With the excess liquid, it is suggested that you dot the various objects in the house such as the stove burners, under the dining room table, T.V., and other heavy objects. Complete the ceremony by dotting all the doors leading into the house and especially the master bedroom door. As your are dotting, enforce the three secrets, using the six true words, along with the ousting hand mudra. Because Realgar is toxic, carefully dispose of the container and also thoroughly wash your hand. If Realgar is not available, use red food coloring. This makes a nice non-toxic substitute.

At the work place, use the same formula as above. Dot your office doors and put three dots on your desk, chair, and computer to unify everything that is a part of your workstation.

Sunshine Buddha Exercise

CHAPTER FOUR
EIGHT ASPECTS OF LIFE

Between the peoples of the world there are common bonds of relationships, wealth, and health. Our priorities may be in different places during various stages of our lives, but essentially we all have basic needs to be met.

In ancient China, the Buddhist priest learned the most auspicious location to bury an ancestor was facing south. South was the direction that was dedicated to fame and rank of his offspring. So important is the correct burial location that a young man once carried the bones of his grandfather for hundreds of miles until he found the ideal burial site. He laid the remains of the old man in a grave with a south-facing river view and a mountain to the back for protection from the harsh winds. As time passed the man rose through the ranks and become the Emperor of China.

There are stories of famous military men and war lords who lost wars because the enemy located and desecrated their ancestors' graves.

Through a complicated system of mathematics, astrology, and geomancy the Buddhists priests designated a specific color, purpose, and anatomy to each of the eight directions.

The eight designated directions are called a gua. Eight guas are referred to as a ba-gua.

South (Li) = fame or rank
South east (Hsun) = wealth or finances
East (Jen) = health or family
North east (Gen) = wisdom
North (Kan) = career
North west (Chyan) = helpful people or travel
West (Dwei) = children or offspring
South west (Kuen) = marriage or relationship

The four traditional schools of Feng Shui use absolute directions and locate these directions with a compass or luopan. The Black Hat school uses the front door which, if in the center, is north or career. Because the stars, moon, and planets are constantly moving, the Black Hat school of thought states that nothing is absolute or stationary.

When arranging a home, the total first floor can be compressed in one ba-gua. As you enter the second floor the head of the staircase is considered the front door or Mouth of Ch'i. Many people choose to arrange each room with a separate super-imposed ba-gua. Each is correct.

If the residents want to activate a special "gua" they can do so in the appropriate section of the total house or in several rooms. For instance, if the residents want to ensure a happy, strong-marriage, they activate the southwest gua with nine stones in a potted plant. The plant can be living or silk. While placing the nine stones, use the three secrets of reinforcement, and visualize a loving, lasting relationship.

To keep the marriage strong, place decorative items, such as a photo of husband and wife in a heart-shaped frame, or pink or red flowers in a white vase in the marriage gua corner of the master bedroom. Wind chimes hung in the marriage gua in the living room will dispense even ch'i throughout the house. If you have a garden, place a large rock or statue in the south west position to represent a solid foundation. It is advised not to plant prickly flowers such as roses or cactus too close to that spot, but you may plant red, yellow, and pink flowers in the gua. They are attractive and increase the flow of ch'i.

If money is your goal, there are several solutions. Locate the south east gua of the house or room. The solutions can be an aquarium with nine fish total,-- either eight red and one black, or eight black and one red (if a fish dies replace it as soon as possible), a red flower in a white vase -- the flower can be real or silk, artificial firecrackers hung from the ceiling, or place a lush green plant in the gua -- if it dies, replace it with a greener and more expensive plant (it is important to groom plants, if there are any dead or dying leaves, remove them immediately).

You may also choose to purchase a non-metallic ring such as jade, coral, hematite, ivory, plastic, ceramic or even a red string. Place the ring under your pillow for nine days. Imagine you are not spending money foolishly or extravagantly. After nine days, place the ring on your middle finger. While doing so express the three secrets using the six sacred words. Repeat the words nine times to cement the ceremony. The appropriate body mudra to use is the "Ousting Mudra."

A healthy road to wealth is the use of fruit because fruit symbolizes prosperity. In the south east gua (wealth) of the kitchen, set a fruit basket or bowl (perhaps one shaped like a boat) on top of a round or octagonal mirror which is larger then the fruit bowl. The kitchen itself generates riches because it is the room that nourishes the inhabitants. If your kitchen is dimly lit, use a higher watt light-bulb to increase and circulate environmental ch'i. Placing a mirror or tin foil behind the burner increases opportunity for prosperity. Follow the adjustment with the three secrets.

The eight trigrams or ba-gua also corresponds to direction, color, parts of the body, and gemstones.

The Feng Shui expert will superimpose the body outline on the floor plan, placing the head north, with the face up. To the experienced eye, determinations can be made as to why residents continue to have certain illnesses or bad luck. After adjusting the objects in the home along with a transcendental cure, there are many miraculous recoveries.

Any other body part not separately listed goes in the center, including heart, lungs, spine, and neck. The colors that correspond with the center are yellow and gold.

Trigram Chart

Direction	Color	Anatomy	Stone	Pathway
S	Red	Eyes	Tiger's Eye, Citrine	Fame or Rank
SE	Blue, Red, or Purple	Hip	Ruby or Red Beryl	Money
E	Green	Foot	Tourmaline	Health
NE	Dark Green, Black, or Blue	Hand	Blue Sapphire or Blue Angelite	Knowledge or Wisdom
N	Black	Ear	Onyx	Career
NW	Black, Gray, or White	Head	Diamond or Clear Quartz	Helpful People and/or Travel
W	White	Mouth	Pearl	Children
SW	White, Pink, or Red	Organs	Pink Tourmaline or Pink Quartz	Marriage or Partnership

CHAPTER FIVE
NINE CURES

Our object is to circulate good energy or ch'i in personal as well as work environment. This in turn brings balance, clarity, good health, and wealth to the residents. What makes negative ch'i? There are several answers some of which include stagnation of ch'i, negative energy vortex, and building on top of old grave yards. The following tools for transformation will rebalance and align a variety of ills. The nine basic cures are divided as follows:

- Light reflecting objects: Mirrors, leaded crystals, electric lights.
- Living objects: Flowers and plants, trees (real or silk), fish tank or aquarium, bonsai tree, bamboo.
- Sounds: Wind chimes, bells, door bell, and tape recorder.
- Electric power items: Record player, computer, T.V., barber poles, running lights, moving sign board.
- Colors: Especially those corresponding to the five elements. Green - wood, red - fire, white - metal, black - water, and yellow or gold - earth.
- Bamboo: Flutes or beaded curtains.
- Moving Objects: Water fountain, mobile, water sprinkler, child's pinwheel, windmill.
- Heavy Objects: Rocks, boulders, statues, desks.
- Other: Five fire crackers, orange peels, fragrance, red ribbons, fringe, rice, chalk and stone lions, and other.

LIGHT REFLECTING OBJECTS: Mirrors are the number one option to fix a stagnant area. Mirrors also are used to increase personal ch'i. If there are noisy neighbors or unpleasant circumstances directed toward you, a mirror properly placed will ward off the evils or annoyances. If traffic passes a house too quickly and it affects the occupant's ch'i, placing a mirror on the outside of the house, on a tree or mailbox will deflect excess ch'i.

There are stories about old China and the "Mirror Wars." At that time every family had a mirror or two in their windows to deflect their neighbors' ch'i. Over time people kept adding more and more mirrors so that their house wouldn't end up with everyone's negative ch'i heaped on it. Things got out of hand and the magistrates had to step in. To keep order they had each home searched for mirrors and only two mirrors were allowed per household.

FACETED CRYSTALS: The crystal could be either quartz or fine cut Austrian crystal. Hang them on a red string or silk ribbon in nine-inch increments. This is a cure for ch'i moving too quickly through a house or hallway. They can be placed on a desk to deflect individual overpowering energy. Many offices use them to deflect the sun's afternoon rays that can drown personnel. The crystal splits the intense sun and attractive multiple rainbows dance through the room. Crystals should be used between a bathroom door jam and the foot of the bed to draw away the commode energy which the Feng Shui experts see as lost opportunities and finances being flushed away through the toilet.

LIGHTING: Is important when entering a home or hallway. Dim lighting can cause headaches and an uneasy feeling. If a house is below the roadway a light on a high pole properly placed will help avoid an ill fate for the occupants. Lighting is important to bring up the ch'i of the occupants. If a light bulb burns out, replace it immediately with a higher wattage.

If a house is odd-shaped and missing a corner, the likely cure is to place a flood light on top of a pole that has been properly placed in the ground to funnel up good ground ch'i. The light should be directed toward the house to symbolically provide the missing corner.

LIVING OBJECTS: Fish are the fruit of the sea; they represent money. Most Asian restaurants have an aquarium to secure profits. If a home doesn't have a view of water, place a fish bowl or aquarium in it. The most auspicious locations are the south east (wealth) or north (career). In places of business, aquariums also double as a means of protection. If a person intending to do harm to the business comes in, his ch'i will be deflected into the aquarium and a fish will die. Replace the fish immediately. The ideal number is nine which symbolizes eternity or strength. Six fish can also be used in a smaller tank.

PLANTS: They represent growth. They also dispense ch'i by varying methods; if the ch'i is stagnant, it will liven it up. If it is too quick it will smooth it out. Plants bring growth along with peace of mind. We all need to see green for our personal mental balance. It is best to use a lush green plan rather than a cactus. As the plants thrive so do the occupants.

SOUNDS: In China brass bells have been used for centuries by shop keepers to protect them from theft. Brass wind chimes are used for balancing ill-shaped rooms. Placed on the back door or gate of a residence, it will bring peace of mind to the occupants, knowing that their house has an effective burglar alarm system. They also attract positive influence to the house. They can attract money and foot traffic to a business.

ELECTRIC POWER ITEMS: Television and computers can be used with the idea of yin and yang balance. For example, movement on the screen is constant but there is a solid base just as it should be in one's career. Place a computer in your north (career) gua. This will enhance your career.

COLORS: To the Chinese, the color white, while it represents purity, also is the color for mourning or death. Red is an auspicious color. It means happiness and life, and this color is used in ceremonies, including the New Year, weddings, and births. Green brings tranquillity, improved health and new growth. Black or dark blue represents money. It should be used sparingly as an accent. If one wishes to sell a house, the ideal colors are white house, yellow trim or shutters, and black roof.

BAMBOO: Flutes made of bamboo are prized especially if they are chunky rather then the long and thin. Bamboo flutes are used to balance ill shaped rooms or obstructions in the house or business. They should be slanted with the mouth piece at the lower end. Place a red silk ribbon around the flute, with one or two red tassels decoratively hanging from the red ribbon. Flutes represent swords. It is the belief of many that they will frighten off evil spirits. They also represent peace and safety to the residents. Many businesses hang a pair of flutes over the cash register as a safety measure.

Beaded curtains are hung on doorways that do not have an actual door. It slows down fast-moving ch'i, especially in long hallways. If a doorway has an arch like a rounded tombstone a beaded curtain will disguise its symbolism of death.

MOVING OBJECTS: Water fountains are the key to healthy finances, but often are not available for home use. A replacement would be a sprinkler system or water sprinkler. Fans or air conditioners are used to circulate stagnant ch'i indoors. A windmill can be used to circulate energy in a missing gua.

Mobiles are used to circulate ch'i in a room. If the mobile has fish on it, it has a two fold benefit because fish represents money. Pinwheels in the garden directed toward the door of entry will stimulate opportunities and bring many people to your door. Windsocks are used in a larger area, such as a missing corner of a house. Carefully placed, a windsock can symbolically make an irregular house shape complete.

HEAVY OBJECTS: To ensure a solid marriage, a rock or statue is placed in the marriage spot to ensure that all is well. When opening a new business or starting a new career a rock in the career gua will anchor the position.

OTHER: It is wise to carry an orange peel in your pocket when visiting a friend at the hospital, or going to a funeral parlor or courthouse. If you are having trouble getting a job or finding a mate, the solution is to cut an orange peel in circles and carry nine circles with you until they dry, then toss them away.

If you prefer not to carry an orange peel for a new job or mate, an alternative solution is to place colorful cut flowers in the master bedroom and kitchen, let them sit there three days, then exchange them for fresh ones. Continue to do this nine consecutive times, total of 27 days.

Firecrackers are used in many ceremonies to scare away ghosts and misguided, mischievous spirits. Symbolic firecrackers can be made out of red paper and a string for a wick. The ideal number is five, placed in a room that needs to uplift its ch'i or in a specific gua. If you need to put energy and excitement back into a relationship place in the south west gua. If your boss isn't giving you the raise you desire, place firecrackers near his picture or business card to make things "pop."

Rice is often used for the conception ritual. Rice is also used to sprinkle around a house or office both inside and outside to feed the homeless spirits. Do this by first scattering the rice to the wind in an upward motion. Then spread the remaining rice, palm down, as if you were planting seeds. This is symbolic of sowing seeds for new growth, which will bring blessings, good luck, and opportunity.

Among the nine basic cures, one or two are used in all transcendental solutions. Use your imagination and adjust a problem with the above solutions or use the "Other" category to suit your needs.

CHAPTER SIX
LOVE & MARRIAGE

When we view the Asian culture, we observe they have a low divorce rate while westerners have a very high rate. Do they know something we don't?

Could it be that most Chinese homes are square or rectangular in shape? These are the most ideal floor plans which traditionally bring the most harmony and least obstacles to the residents.

There are various reasons why a marriage is not succeeding.

1. House Shape
2. Exposed Ceiling Beams in Bedroom
3. Bed Placement
4. House Entrance
5. Color of Interior
6. Kitchen Stove Placement
7. Slanted Walls
8. Narrow Staircase
9. Projecting Corners
10. Pictures on Wall
11. Furniture Arrangement
12. Personal Ch'i
13. Roadway too Close to House (Glaring Car Lights)
14. Shape of Property Line
15. Rickety or Crooked Porch or Entrance

The Feng Shui expert first looks at the shape of the house. If the house is U-shaped with the master bedroom in the front, this leads to one or both spouses eating or sleeping away from home. To rectify this problem, move the master bedroom away from the U-location and place it at the back of the house. Plant shrubs to form a visual rectangle, in the front of the house or place a mirror opposite the bedroom door to draw the U-shaped wing back to the main part of the house for completion.

If the house is boot-shaped and the bedroom is located at the tip or toe of the boot, the marriage is stubbing its toe. Either move the bedroom or hang a mirror so that it reflects the bed away from the sole.

Beams can be a dilemma because they cut through communication. If two people talk with a beam overhead, neither are certain of what the other stated. The beam acts like a separator; it causes an invisible wall between them. A beam positioned lengthwise over a bed separates the sleepers, which in turn, will separate the marriage. To resolve this obstacle, the bed could be moved to another location, fringe could be hung from the beam to soften its heaviness, an attractive mobile could be fastened above the bed, or two flutes with red ribbon wrapped around them could be placed on the beams with their mouthpieces angled downward to make a ba-gua.

Bed placement is of vital importance. As mentioned previously, it is a bad omen to have the foot of the bed directly in front of the door. If moving the bed is not an option, place a faceted crystal between the foot of the bed and doorway. Placing the bed in the marriage corner (south west) is the most auspicious. It is always important to see the threshold of the room. Position a mirror so there is a clear view of the door if it is obstructed. The ch'i of the occupant is startled if people entering aren't easily seen. This can cause nervousness or grumpiness. This can lead to arguing over trivial matters.

If you enter the house through the garage door, this can cloud one's thinking. If there are three or four doors to pass through before getting to the living room, this is referred to as "The Heart Piercing Door." It can cause quarrels, insomnia, or eye problems. To circumvent these hazards, use another door to enter the house or hang a brass wind chime or mirror between the second and third door. Doors misaligned are another problem; hang a mirror on the opposite door or hang a crystal ball between the two doors. This will smooth out the energy.

Color plays an important role in harmony in one's surroundings. Red is auspicious but too much red can encourage quarrels. Family rooms and bedrooms should have restful colors. Is the wall paper too busy? Select a more subtle, relaxing pattern. Green shades allow the mind to rest and the body to regenerate. Add touches of plants near staircases. Yellow accents will bring a sunny cheerful feeling. Lighting will lift up the occupant's ch'i; dark colors can be depressing.

If the stove faces away from the entry door and the cook is not able to see who is behind her, she gets unnerved. Her emotions go into the food and arguments begin. Put a mirror above the stove so the entrance is in clear view.

Slanted walls will lower the occupant's ch'i. It can generate depression or lack of confidence. This makes a marriage shaky. Place a plant in a shiny reflective pot or install a mirror along the slant to uplift the room ch'i and bring balance to the other wall. A floor lamp would also lift up and circulate room ch'i.

When one walks up a narrow staircase, it makes the person feel uneasy. Short of replacing the total staircase, have a long light on the ceiling to brighten the path and ideally a mirror on the landing or at the top of the stairs.

Projecting corners emit what is termed as "Killer Ch'i." These are objects pointing toward the residents. If the furniture is arranged with corners facing another chair or bed, rearrange the furniture into a more rounded form. If it's a protruding wall or some other heavy object, hang or put a planter in front of it or block the projection with a screen.

If pictures or paintings appear angry, depressing or have signs of death in them, they should be exchanged for flowers, happy people, birth, or growth.

There can be external influences such as the road being too close to the house. Glaring lights shining in the bedroom during the night can cause restlessness in one's sleep. To prevent this from diminishing one's life force, hang black-out draperies or place a weather vane facing traffic. A mirror placed inside on the window ledge facing traffic will deflect the excess road ch'i. The most ideal cure is to move the bedroom to the rear of the house. This will give the residents more power and calm their nerves.

Before going to a lawyer for a divorce, it would be wise and less expensive to have a Feng Shui consultant inspect your living quarters to determine the root of the conflict. Many couples saved their marriages by adjusting home ills and using transcendental cures.

The room adjustment can also be imagined. Use mental visualization and place yourself in the center of a selected room. You will actually feel yourself moving if the room is not in total balance. You can mentally arrange the room and see if it is balanced. When you physically return to the room, carry out your adjustments.

Ideally, the furniture of a room should be grouped in the form of the eight-sided ba-gua. Planters and mobiles can replace a piece of furniture. Angling screens, pictures, or lamps also add to the ba-gua.

Most important, do the "Three Secrets" during or after any adjustments. This then cements the transcendental cure and propels it into reality and success.

Flutes on Beam Create Ba-gua

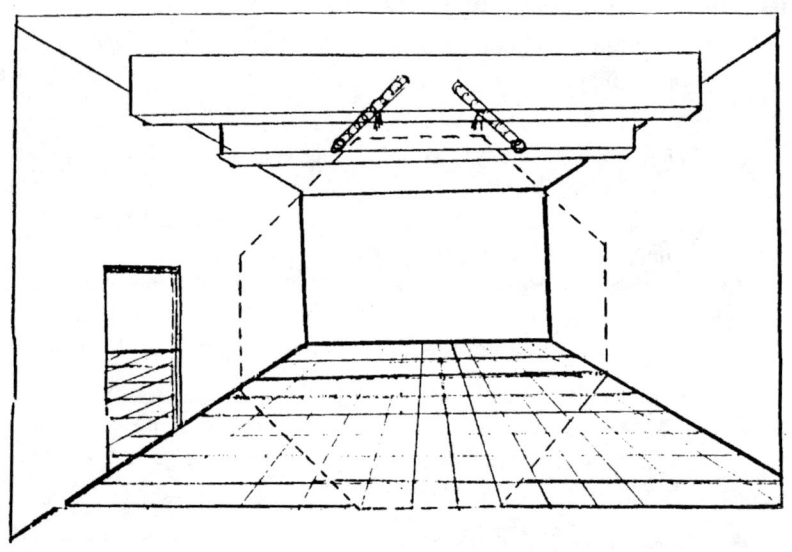

CHAPTER SEVEN
HOME AND HEALTH

In selecting a plot of land, certain land sites are more desirous than others. The best are square, rectangular, round, semi-circle, purse shape (narrow in front wide in rear) and friendly animal shape i.e. camel or clam. It is wise to place the house in the center of the plot for more balance. The land shapes that cause problems if not adjusted by Feng Shui manipulations are the following: triangular, arrow shape, long and narrow, especially dust pan shape; if wide in front and narrow in rear.

House shapes have a direct relationship with its residents. For instance, health, wealth, balance, and communication are all tied into the house shape and internal room placement. The door represents the mouth, windows eyes, and hallways are the veins and arteries. To adjust the ch'i of the house superimpose the trigram (ba-gua) using the front door (if in the center) as the north direction. It is north east to the far left and north west to the far right. See where there is vacant space or an empty gua. Use one or more of the nine cures to guide you in readjusting the house or apartment and employ the three secrets to cement them into place.

The U-shape house often causes one of the spouses to sleep away from home and or eat out. Cleaver-shape causes accidents and opportunities gone astray. L-shaped houses are missing a gua. The front door will determine which gua is missing. To remedy this, place a light pole with the light directed towards the vacant gua to connect the house visually, or plant shrubs and/or flowers to visually enclose the gua.

A boot shape is a modified L. A bedroom in the toe will make occupants accident prone. A cleaver shape is similar. You are cutting opportunities away. It can also cause arguments and a razor sharp tongue to those around you. This can lead to divorce and loss of business. Personal injury will befall those sleeping on the blade side. Install a large mirror on the opposite wall to draw in the edge. It is advisable to move the bedroom to the handle part of house.

A house too close to a church will have sad times. Plant trees to block the view, or place a mirror in windows to face the church. A tall building next door to the house will stunt growth, health, and career for the residents. Place a convex mirror directly at the building to overshadow its massive size.

Home interiors can bring opportunities and happiness or plague its residents with a variety of struggles and illnesses. Three doors or windows in a row can cause conflict or quarrels among family members. An aquarium or fish bowl near the windows is the cure recommended, or hang a crystal between the doorways to defuse the strong ch'i.

A staircase if too close to the front entry will cause money to flow out of the home. Put a planter at bottom of stairs, and full length mirror at top, or a crystal ball next to last step. If there is a staircase going up next to another going down this will cause stubbornness, leading to misunderstanding. Place a large, lush, green plant or small tree at the junction of staircases along with a wind chime, and wrap the banister with green silk vines. Stairways should be wide and well lit. Otherwise the residents will feel unsettled and careers will be diminished.

Spiral staircases are like a corkscrew that can cause physical illnesses, usually affecting the head and midline, frequently causing headaches, heart palpitations, diseases of the organs or miscarriages, and anxiety. Master Lin stated "never build a spiral staircase in a existing house or you are asking for a tidal wave of woes." Several transcendental solutions are i.e. paint the stairs blue or green, wind green silk or plastic around the banister and position an overhead light with high wattage over the staircase to illuminate it and increase ch'i circulation.

Narrow stairs leading to a house or apartment, limit the residents' opportunities and advancements. Place shrubs or flowers on both sides of the stairs (anything prickly should not be used), or install lamps on pedestals to brighten the pathway.

Bookshelves if too tall and piled to the top near the ceiling can cause headaches - especially in a small room. The basic cure is to have some books standing and a few on their sides to create the yin-yang effect. Don't have books on the higher shelves unless they are in small groupings with a few attractive nic-nacks to brake up the massiveness.

A house below street level will diminish career opportunities and the residents will not be seen or heard by others. Therefore, their requests will go unheeded. Funnel the earth's ch'i by way of a tall flag pole behind the house or use a windsock, light pole, or a revolving roof fan.

Seeing the bathroom first when one enters the house is bad Feng Shui. Its ominous meaning is money flushing away. If a bathroom is in the center of the house, career, health and money will suffer. The solution is to hang mirrors on all four walls in the bathroom (they need not be large) or wallpaper with shiny foil paper, (silver color is best). Health problems will occur if the bathroom and kitchen are next to each other, especially digestive disorders and ulcers. A faceted crystal will defuse the environmental ch'i. If the commode is visible, conceal it with a hanging plant, towel rack, or screen. A small mirror on the outside of the door is an appropriate adjustment, or hang a small wind chime near the inside of the door. You could wallpaper the ceiling with foil paper to have a reflective effect (appears to bring water up). If you are designing the home hide the commode with a partition. If there is a bath room connected to the master bedroom it can cause a multiple of ills. If the toilet is positioned where the residents' midlines are while they sleep, they could suffer from abdominal or intestinal problems. Cure: hang a faceted crystal between the foot of the bed and the outside of the bathroom door. Bathrooms at the end of a long hallway are problematic in that they can cause intestinal and/or reproductive ailments. Cure: suspend a mobile in the hallway to circulate excess fast ch'i. In addition, if your decor allows, hang a beaded curtain on the outside of door.

Beams are attractive and are used in an open house design. If there are many beams we discount them. If there are two or three in a room they can be the secret culprit to problems. If a visible beam divides a table beneath it those who are dining will not clearly understand the other party (miscommunication). Beams in a bedroom can cause physical ailments. A beam directly over the head can cause headaches; across the abdomen, stomach diseases such as ulcers. If over the feet it tends to make one home bound and or have weak ankles. If it divides the sleepers it will eventually separate the marriage. Cure: hang a scalloped red tassel or fringe across the length of the beam to soften its massiveness. Or hang a mobile or faceted crystal on the beam to deflect its appearance. The best solution is to move the bed between beams for a feeling of security. A cure all is to hang two bamboo flutes at an angle with the mouthpieces facing downward on the beam to complement the room with an illusionary ba-gua (see diagram on page 26).

If a house is extended one half or less of the width, it is very beneficial. It adds to the gua. For example, if there is an addition in the marriage area it will increase marital bliss. If in children gua, there may be many births and the children should be healthy and successful in life. Sometimes the children's gua refers to birthing an idea or product. If in the helpful people/travel gua, one's needs will be met or expect to travel frequently.

Trees are a wonderful means to disguise many architectural irregularities. Proper placement of these trees, however, is essential. For example, having trees too close to the front door is not beneficial as this can block one's career advancement. If you have an existing tree within three feet of the front door, either place a small mirror at eye level on the tree or a mobile to circulate nature's ch'i. If there is a dead tree in front of the house, remove it. It is bad luck, especially for older residents.

The location of the residence is vital. If the house is at the end of a dead end street or cul de sac, excess ch'i will enter the house. This will create nervousness, quick temper, and stress for the residents. Cure: direct a weather vane towards oncoming traffic; trees can also be used to shield the traffic. If the house is on a hairpin turn, the bedroom should be located away from oncoming traffic, and a wall should be built as a safety shield with reflective lights on the traffic side.

A house is most safe when in the middle of the block. Houses on corners are targets for robbers. Cure: Use the silent alarm system, and place bells on the back of the door or the patio gate. The sound will ward off a would-be robber.

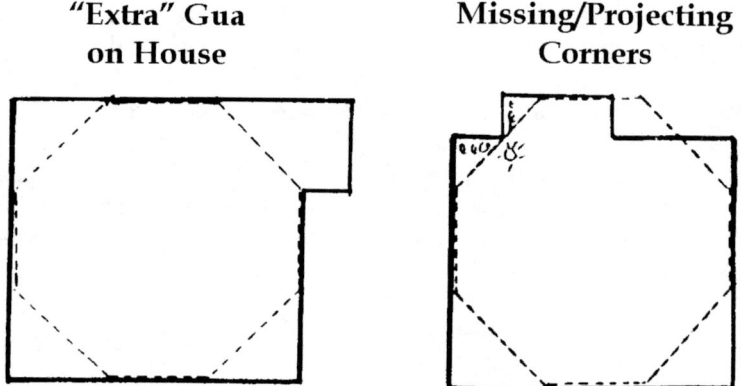

"Extra" Gua on House

Missing/Projecting Corners

CHAPTER EIGHT
BUSINESS

Many U.S. and Canadian firms have offices in the far east. Before a business can open its doors, the Asian employees insist that a Feng Shui consultant first inspect the premises. While some westerners may not believe in the system they do so to keep their staff content. Every bank in Taiwan, Hong Kong and Singapore used Feng Shui principles to bring in business and make its customers feel confident that their money is secure.

Most banks have a fish tank or aquarium in the lobby, as mentioned earlier. Fish are a sign of prosperity and wealth. Touches of red, green, and gold or yellow will be noticed in the decor. The red is for prosperity, green for growth and gold or yellow for the center of activity (it symbolizes the sun).

If a business isn't able to place a fish tank without it looking awkward, a water dispenser in a five-gallon jug set in the south east corner of the room would have the same auspicious results. A picture of the ocean or fishermen with filled nets would enhance such a room.

It isn't auspicious to have an escalator descending directly toward the entrance. This is viewed as money and prospects leaving too quickly. There are several cures for this situation. If this is found in a store, place a display case between the door and the escalator. This will trap and recirculate much of the ch'i. A cut or faceted crystal suspended from the ceiling will slow the ch'i. A final cure would be to have a bamboo curtain or a screen by the door. Some businesses have set bamboo planters on either side of the escalator so that their customers' attention is distracted from the location of the entrance as they descend.

If two people share an office, it would be ideal to have their desks face the door, set kitty-corner from each other to form a ba-gua. This avoids arguments and increases harmony.

If an office is at the end of a long hallway, the occupant is likely to receive too much ch'i. This could cause stress, jumpiness, or workaholism. Several ideas to tone the ch'i down are: place a faceted crystal on the desk in view of the hallway; a rabbit figurine could also be used - they are known for their quickness; a statue of a baseball catcher is effective, or a large hour glass filled with sand.

Be cautious of narrow zig zagging hallways. They are notorious for unbalancing the ch'i of those individuals who use them, resulting in arguing, loss of creative spirit, and other negative repercussions.

A young executive may want to secure his or her career by having a rock or statue in the office placed in the north gua position. This will insure a solid career. If placed in the south gua position, fame or moving up the ranks is implied. For extra good fortune use both spots!

Black Hat school of Feng Shui utilizes both traditional implements as well as modern. Computers play an important role in daily business. There is a constant source of energy moving through the computer and screen. The movement raises the ch'i of the operator and stimulates the operator's knowledge. When arranging one's office decide in which gua it will supply the most needed ch'i. If you are a writer, you may want it in the fame or helpful people sections. If you need to sell the product of the computer's work, choose the wealth gua. Add a mobile or something that moves to get things going. Hang a planter above the computer for growth in your selected field. The computer will deliver the ch'i to make it happen.

When selecting a place of business do not choose a location near a funeral parlor, church, or, even worse, an established route to a cemetery. It is less than ideal to be near stagnant water. If the neighborhood has had a number of robberies, businesses closing up, or freak accidents, be aware of them. Frankly, it is advised always to perform the "Sealing the Door" ceremony, followed by the three secrets, to disassociate your business from those previously located there.

If you take over an office after the previous occupant has been promoted, that is good ch'i. If you inherit an office because of a demotion or firing, be warned the same circumstance may befall you. The office should be changed around a bit. Hang a different picture on the wall, bring in a green plant and put nine stones in the plant pot. As you do so, visualize you are rooting yourself to your job. Place a mirror on your desk or face up in your desk drawer to ward off the evil eye. You might even try the "Sealing the Door" ceremony to rid old ch'i.

Don't sit with your back to a window with direct sunlight. You will be viewed in outline and not as a whole person and you will lose power. A safety measure is to have your desk chair at least three feet from the wall. Otherwise you will weaken your position of power if you are too close.

If the desk is near the door, you will often lose your concentration at the end of the work day or just leave early. The door makes you think of going home. To avoid this conduct, place a mirror on the opposite wall so your attention will be distracted away from the door.

Never sit with your back to a door. Psychologically and physically, ill will befall you. You are in a powerless spot and you will be startled whenever someone comes up behind you. This causes lack of concentration and productivity. If the work space can't be turned, position a mirror to see who is entering and leaving.

The optimum location for the top executive or supervisor's office is farthest from the main entrance of the building or the specific department. That person needs to be spared the distraction of incidentals going on. The positioning will put this person at a point of concentration and authority. Desk placement should be diagonally from the door.

We can learn from Chinese restaurants. Most have an aquarium, green plants, and a mirror behind the bar to double the conviviality not to mention the profits. Very often a mirror, well placed behind the cash register will symbolize doubled profits. Place a red flower in a white vase near the cash register or what is considered the profit area. The vase will symbolize peace (the white) and (the red) life line for better profits.

Care is given to the design of the tables and chairs, especially the largest, or family table which has an octagon shape. The ba-gua is beneficial for the owner and customer alike. The patrons who join in a communal meal feel balanced, which leads to good digestion, meaningful conversation, and unity as a group. Chair backs are usually solid to indicate a supportive environment.

When you want the advantage of power on your side, do the following: sit in a chair with a solid back. Your chair should be a little taller then your client's chair. Wear solid colors, a small pattern in a tie is O.K., and do not have a lot of nic-nacks behind you (they cause distractions). If there is a window behind you, draw the drapes so as not to cause a distraction. Quiet music will assist concentration and relaxation. Cut flowers or a healthy green plant on, or in back of, the desk will bring life to the meeting or contract.

CHAPTER NINE
WEALTH & PROSPERITY

Prosperity is not a happenstance, but clever engineering to acquire earthly goods.

When selecting a homesite, remember the south east is the direction of wealth. It is a fact that in the city of Denver, Colorado, there are more wealthy people in the south-east area than any other district.

The color red is auspicious, either as a red brick house or a red flagstone walkway up to the front door. Fill your garden with red and yellow flowers in a flowing pattern. Avoid points, coffin or tombstone shapes. Evergreens on the property line will secure longevity. Don't plant trees near the front door otherwise in time it will block career opportunities. Be cautioned not to have trees of any type too close to windows. An obstructed view can inhibit the gua's purpose.

If you live in an apartment building, it is advisable to be several floors above the traffic's noise. It isn't good to live on the top floor because it lacks a feeling of strong foundation. The center floors are the wisest choice.

Square columns can be an obstacle; if the columns are round they aren't as much as a deterrent. Hang a mirror toward the top of the column or drape green foliage around it to mask the sharp corners. This will recycle the environmental ch'i.

Furniture design is important. A roll-top desk has both yin and yang qualities. This is very good. Select a solid back chair; it will support your career decisions. Have all team members at work sit in solid-backed chairs for congruity.

I have a ba-gua shaped calculator in the south east corner of my desk. This auspicious design multiplies money!

Restaurants and small shops should not place the cash register in front of the Mouth of Ch'i; have it diagonally set, with a mirror facing the register to double profits.

Recently, I had a meal at a local Korean restaurant. They had a huge aquarium in the center of the room. These wise business people aren't taking any chances. They tied all eight guas together. Like a wheel they wanted their business to roll smoothly down the road to success.

Often Asian executives will have a rooster feather hidden in a desk drawer to protect against someone figuratively stabbing them in the back or spreading spurious stories to discredit their business.

Most men like trophies to grace their walls. Be forewarned that a dead animal head or body is blocking ch'i. Asians never keep reminders of death or objects shaped like coffins, tombstones or two incense sticks in their immediate surroundings. If you must have it in your office or home carefully decide which gua is currently least important. Instead you may prefer to display pictures or a sculpture of fishermen pulling in full nets, a boat heading toward the harbor, or an ocean scene (but not an ocean storm, the bad weather will influence your career). A properly placed bamboo flute with a red tassel will symbolically shelter you and your business. The flute signifies both a sword and peace.

If you are a shopkeeper, consider getting a moving electrical sign to catch the eye of pedestrian traffic. This has replaced the old-fashioned barber pole. A red sidewalk, carpeting, or awning will entice customers in. Add brass wind chimes at the door entrance. The sound will attract customers. On a slow day stimulate business by scattering birdseed at the main entrance. Birds circulate good ch'i by their fluttering wings. Squawking birds should be avoided. Hummingbirds are a very auspicious sign. Business will hum along with a hummingbird feeder.

Aquariums are synonymous with money. If placed in the following locations it will route money to you. Here are several examples. Kan (north) = career, Dwei (west) = children may receive a scholarship, Li (south) = fame/rank or promotion, Gen (northeast) = knowledge, selling your ideas or invention.

A pond or swimming pool can be the ticket to bringing in money from the back of the house. A kidney-shaped pool is a good choice if it curves toward the house. A hot tub, especially octagon-shaped, is a popular solution. Choose either the fame or wealth gua for this cure. You can also use a fountain to stimulate wealth in front of your business. Place on a dragon point if you can. Dragon points are rich green patches of grass. Water sprinklers are also effective. If business is slow call home and have the maid turn on the water sprinkler in the wealth and or helpful gua. Avoid stagnant water because it stagnates your opportunities.

If dealing with a large volume of water, it is best to have your house or business face the water. This placement will allow the waves to roll toward the building.

Remember, the house is always the beginning of prosperity. It is the extension of one's self. A happy home is projected into the business. If you hire a Feng Shui consultant to inspect your business, it is best to have them first inspect your home. Many wise business people went the extra mile and also had their secretaries or office manager's homes also inspected and adjusted to make a very successful winning team.

The pig in the Chinese zodiac means money. To accumulate more money toss coins of a certain denomination into a piggy-bank daily. It should be positioned either in hsun gua (south east), or under your bed directly under your right hand. Toss the coins in daily for either 27, 99, or 109 days. Enforce them with the "Three Secrets" nightly.

Visualize Your Goals

CHAPTER TEN
CHINESE ZODIAC

The Chinese zodiac differs from western astrology. Instead of defining the signs by the twelve months as we do, the Chinese base theirs on a cycle of twelve years, according to each lunar year. The animals are in the following order: dragon, snake, horse, goat or ram, monkey, cock or rooster, dog, pig, rat, ox or bull, tiger and rabbit. Each also symbolizes a two hour period of strength, luck or best advantage. If your personal hours are at an inconvenient time, look at your compatible sign's hours to suit your schedule.

THE OX: 1901, 1913, 1925, 1937, 1949, 1961, 1973, 1985, 1997.
Time: 1 a.m.- 3 a.m.
The Ox has a natural tendency to help others and fight for a cause. They are hard working and usually patient. This person can be stubborn and slow to change his or her mind.

THE TIGER: 1902, 1914, 1926, 1938, 1950, 1962, 1974, 1986, 1998.
Time: 3 a.m.- 5 a.m.
Has natural leadership qualities. Shows courage and others admire their self-assurances. Open minded to new ideas and acts on them. This big cat can resist authority.

THE RABBIT: 1903, 1915, 1927, 1939, 1951, 1963, 1975, 1987, 1999.
Time: 5 a.m.- 7 a.m.
The rabbit is quick and sensitive to the point of holding a grudge. They are clever, and aloof. Good luck is on their side. Gets side tracked and doesn't finish projects.

THE DRAGON: 1904, 1916, 1928, 1940, 1952, 1964, 1976, 1988, 2000.
Time: 7 a.m.- 9 a.m.
The dragon has an interest in alchemy and possesses magical abilities and skills. They are shrewd and energetic and lucky at new adventures. Short term personal relationships are common. Often marriages do not work out.

THE SNAKE: 1905, 1917, 1929, 1941, 1953, 1965, 1977, 1989, 2001.
Time: 9 a.m.- 11 a.m.
Snakes are understanding of other's woes and are wise in counsel. Good at decision making, plans, and are studious and need their space. They are sometimes fickle and selfish.

THE HORSE: 1906, 1918, 1930, 1942, 1954, 1966, 1978, 1990, 2002.
Time: 11 a.m.- 1 p.m.
Hard-working and loyal, the Horse is good at making money. Usually charming, this person can want his or her own way.

THE RAM: 1907, 1919, 1931, 1943, 1955, 1967, 1979, 1991, 2003.
Time 1 p.m.- 3 p.m.
The Ram is easy-going, artistic, good at business. Unfortunately this animal is often sullen and not family-oriented.

THE MONKEY: 1908, 1920, 1932, 1944, 1956, 1968, 1980, 1992, 2004.
Time: 3 p.m.- 5 p.m.
Funny, enjoyable, a good problem-solver, and outstanding in business, self-righteous and frequently boastful of accomplishments. The monkey has been known to be lazy.

THE COCK: 1909, 1921, 1933, 1945, 1957, 1969, 1981, 1993, 2005.
Time 5 p.m.- 7 p.m.
Good company, hard-working and resourceful. There can be an element of self-righteousness.

THE DOG: 1910, 1922, 1934, 1946, 1958, 1970, 1982, 1994, 2006.
Time: 7 p.m.- 9 p.m.
The Dog is faithful, honest, and likes to be on the cutting edge of what's happening. Carries nervous energy and acts defensive. Enjoys planning the next venture.

THE PIG: 1911, 1923, 1935, 1947, 1959, 1971, 1983, 1995, 2007.
Time: 9 p.m.- 11 p.m.
Intelligent and cultured, the pig is also caring. Lucky but lazy, these people need someone to fight their battles.

THE RAT: 1912, 1924, 1936, 1948, 1960, 1972, 1984, 1996, 2008.
Time: 11 p.m.- 1 a.m.
The rat is charming and meticulous; they lose focus and change homes and jobs often. They can be greedy and lean toward gambling. The most famous rat is Mickey Mouse.

For a list of complement signs to yours and others which are not compatible refer to page 10.

CHAPTER ELEVEN
TESTIMONIALS

Since I began my practice as a Feng Shui consultant, I kept files on my clients. I have also talked with a friend who shared some of her case histories with me. My friend, Iris Kinney of Dallas, Texas, is a professional astrologer and practices both Black Hat and traditional Feng Shui with an emphasis on western and eastern astrology.

While visiting a holistic clinic I was told it was on the verge of closing. As I glanced around I noticed several deviations which diminished the clinic's ch'i. I suggested that a mobile be hung so that it would offset a slanted wall, placing a mirror at the entrance, and turning the massage table toward the room's east direction to encourage wellness. The changes were made and several days later, business picked up. The owner of the clinic firmly believes that Feng Shui saved her business.

A Denver psychic had to move and didn't have the extra money to do so. She called and asked how to reach this goal. I told her to hang a nine-inch red ribbon in the south east (wealth gua) of her office and aim a small fan at it to circulate stagnant energy. Over the next two days she had seven paying clients. Two days later a friend gave her a much-needed car. The following week she found a mobile home for sale much below market value. She bought it and began moving in. The woman had a helper but on the last and most important day, he was unavailable. She called again to seek a solution and I told her to move the red ribbon to the north east (helpful people) and set the fan near it to stimulate motion. In two hours her ex-husband called to see how she was doing and ended up helping her complete the move.

Putting crystals and gem stones in the appropriate gua helped a Denver businessman triple his business in a few months. He was able to buy a new home for his growing family while keeping the first house for a rental.

A Wichita, Kansas, executive was having trouble collecting on his accounts. After inspecting his home I noted his bed was in the center of the bedroom. The bed placement symbolized an aimlessly floating raft. We discussed the options available to him by repositioning the bed. The head of the bed needs to be against a wall for the foundation of life's aspects. He choose the wealth sector (south east) wall. Soon after he secured a substantial contract with the added bonus of marriage to his sweetheart.

A friend who was overstocked with inventory placed an octagon mirror in the south east (wealth) corner of her office. Three days later, the phone started ringing with orders. On one day alone, she sold ten percent of her inventory. She became a true believer of Feng Shui.

I had the opportunity to be a consultant for an independent clothing manufacturer when he was preparing to move into a new factory. Appropriate colors were chosen for the walls and the department locations were decided according to the Feng Shui principles. The plant manager's office was placed farthest from the main entrance and his desk was set kitty-corner from the door. The Sealing of the Door and Sprinkling of Rice ceremonies were performed. The owner went the extra mile and on opening day fired off five fire crackers and arranged for the mayor to cut a (red) ribbon at the front of the building. All is well and the business is thriving.

A chiropractor hired me to fix his sluggish business. A long hallway moved ch'i through too quickly. A mobile or faceted crystal was recommended to slow the ch'i down in the hallway. This worked to the doctor's advantage. Pen drawings on the wall were nice but the gray frames around the black and white illustrations were too bland. I suggested a picture of flowers or a boat coming toward the shore. The doctor's private office had a prized stuffed deer head in his career corner. Although the man saw it as a trophy, as a Feng Shui practitioner I saw it as a dead head bringing little or no opportunity. It needed to be removed. The office staff had set a prickly cactus near the payment window. It unsettled the patients' ch'i. Over a few weeks time, adjustments were made and his business improved.

A well known country-western singer contacted Iris Kinney for an answer to his dilemma. He hadn't had a hit record for many years and most of his new ventures were failures. Iris inspected his home and spotted an antique sword hanging above his records in his office. The sword was removed because it symbolized cutting his career and opportunities in half. The sword was replaced with a flute and that, along with a few other adjustments, set the man's personal ch'i in motion. Within a few weeks the singer was back on track with singing engagements and writing marketable songs.

An artist attended a class and now sees a new dimension of art and interior art design using the five elements and specific gua placement.

Disturbed by unexpected marital problems, a couple in Dallas asked Iris for direction. She walked through their home and found two striking irregularities. The window screens in the master bedroom had been ripped by a storm months earlier and the swimming pool, which was beneath their bedroom, was stagnant and had green moss growing in it. The couple was instructed to repair the screens, which represented the marriage foundation being torn apart, and clean up the pool, which represented the marriage as being stagnant and sinking. Soon the union regained its original warmth.

A young woman, upset that her boyfriend had moved to Hollywood, California, to seek his fame and fortune, appealed to Iris for help. The woman hadn't heard from the man in a month. She was told to put his picture in the (marriage) corner with rabbits in front of it and to put hearts or a Valentine's card next to the bunnies. Once the transcendental cure was in place, the errant boyfriend called the next day, and returned home.

My friend in financial need tosses bird seed on the pathway from the street to her home when business is slow. The birds eating the seed cause movement and stir the stagnant ch'i. Within 24 hours business always picks up.

I found a silver hubcap near a pot hole. I set it up against a tree on my patio which is in the south east gua. Within days, a land fall of business came in. Round, silver, objects represent coins and the tree is a foundation. This is a simple effective cure.

A friend placed a red rose in a white vase as I had advised. Three days later the Social Security office contacted her. They had over-looked a check due her for over $3,000 dollars.

A lady wanted to travel. She placed a small tree in the north west gua (travel). Then she decorated the tree with travel folders. In less then one year, she had traveled to Hawaii, England, and the Caribbean.

A doctor consulted with me regarding his office personnel; they were uncooperative with each other causing stress and disharmony. I suggested several ways to recirculate the ch'i with a simple and attractive way to separate their desks. Harmony was restored and everyone worked as a team.

In 1992, I performed a balancing in the marriage corner in a lady's home. One year later she invited me to attend her wedding. I took a piece of the wedding cake home. I placed it in my relationship gua and the next year I got married.

My new husband attended one of my Feng Shui classes and learned how to strengthen his relationship gua. He took my name and put it on a valentine heart. Two months later he asked me to marry him and I said yes.

A friend had a financial problem. I suggested a fish tank be placed in her helpful people gua. Within a few days, she started receiving referrals from other customers and her money began to flow.

A young couple was having a power struggle in their business. They both wanted to be the boss. After attending a Feng Shui lecture, they went home and assessed their house. The first item they saw upon entering the house was a power breaker. They determined this was the key to their power struggle. After camouflaging the power box, they equally shared in the responsibilities of their business. It made their lives less stressful and more productive.

While visiting a neighbor, I noticed a large ceramic frog outside his door. I made a statement that frogs are generally bad luck. The next day he tossed all the ceramic frogs into the trash. Two days later his business was better then ever.

When business gets slow, we now spritz Abundance oil on our telephone, business cards and ourselves. Of course we always recite the "Three Secrets" and visualize business picking up. It never fails - the phone starts ringing within 30 to 45 minutes.

While visiting the Southeast I rented a car. The car was brand new and only had a paper sticker on the back window. This concerned me, because of frequent robberies of cars. I dotted the car daily with White Angelica oil. I felt confident that I would not have any trouble and I didn't.

Friends needed to sell their California home due to a job transfer. The real estate market was slow and prices were dropping. A Feng Shui consultant was called in to resolve this complex problem. After several minor but significant adjustments, the house was put on the market and sold in one day. A square pillar inside the house close to the front door was blocking the flow of ch'i entering the house. The owner easily corrected the problem by hanging a green leafy plant on each side of the pillar. This softened the corners of the pillar and facilitated the flow of ch'i.

The key to Feng Shui is to bring man in balance with his environment. This can be done by strengthening the gua energies.

GLOSSARY

Alchemy An ancient technique used to manipulate energies.

Astrology Chinese astrology utilizes animals and employs a lunar year calendar. Different animals represent a series of twelve years.

Ba-gua An octagonal shape which represents the eight avenues of life, i.e., health, wealth, children.

Ch'i Universal energy often called cosmic breath. It is further divided into various forms including: house ch'i, personal ch'i, environmental ch'i, and land ch'i. Without ch'i, there is no life.

Feng Shui Geomancy, meaning wind and water. It brings balance to environments through furniture placement so man is in balance with his Universe and personal surroundings. It removes obstacles and replaces life's hurdles with luck and smoother passage.

Four Animals The four animals which represent the cardinal directions are: azure dragon East, white tiger West, red bird South, and black tortoise North.

Front Door The front door is considered north if in the center of the entry, NE to the far left and NW to the far right. Absolute directions are not used with Black Hat F.S.

Secret Arrows Bad Feng Shui, harmful object or situations that can unsettle one's personal ch'i.

Sacred Words Six sacred words are: **"Om Ma Ni Pad Me Hum"** which means, "The jewel in the center of the heart beats in the center of the Universe." Should be recited nine times when making a Feng Shui adjustment.

Yin-Yang Universal balance through opposition, i.e., light-dark, earth-heavens, man-woman, quiet-expressive, hard-soft.

FENG SHUI ITEMS

There are a variety of articles that can enhance or help the serious minded Feng Shui practitioner, student or interested individual. Most of these cannot be found in stores.

Postage & handling (p/h) for coin/charm/fish: Add $1.50 for 1; $1.90 for 2; $2.20 for 3; and $.25 for each additional.

A. Feng Shui Book
  Health Wealth and Balance Through Feng Shui by E.J. Finster $6.49
  + $1.25 p/h

B. Longevity & Peaceful Tranquility Charm (small brass charm)
  especially good for older people...$2.50

C. Happiness and Longevity Coin (Chinese wine bottle shape).............................$3.00

D. Business Good Luck & Conquering Obstacles Coin
  Some say it ensures a continual flow of business...$3.50

E. Good Luck in Business Round Charm
  size 14mm or heart shape w/ bow & jump ring 16mm......................................$2.00

F. Gambling & Prosperity Chinese Charm (10mm x 15mm – tower shape)
  Place in wallet or cash register..$2.50

G. Spirit Protection, Ba-Gua Shape (8 sided) Coin
  with I Ching symbols used to deflect the evil eye from home/business..................$3.50
  Tiny Ba-Gua Shape Charm with Jump-Ring (14mm)
  with I Ching and Yin-Yang symbols..$2.00

H. Chinese Small Yin-Yang Round Coin (1" or 25mm size)
  for attracting money and focus..6/$5.00
  + $1.95 p/h
  Chinese Medium Yin-Yang Round Coin (1½")..$3.00
  Chinese Extra-Large Yin-Yang Round Coin (2" with phoenix & dragon)............$4.00

I. "Kill the Devil" Octagon Shape with Figure of Warrior with Sword (1⅛")
  Place in a car or above door for protection...$3.75

J. Round Coin (1¼" wide) For the family of 5 generations, to bring health, happiness, and protection, put under table..$3.75

K. KU-Yin Coin the Chinese (1⅛" wide)
  "Goddess of Compassion" and protection octagon shaped................................$3.50

L. Heart-Shape Charm with "Double Happiness" Symbol (11mm)
  It's meaning to double fortune, love or luck..$2.00

M. Zodiac Round Coin (55mm)
  Chinese lettering with animal shape, near center is I Ching symbols hole in center.........$3.75

N. Heart Shaped with Bamboo Figure on Charm
  for new babies, or new beginnings, of marriage or business............................$2.00

O. **Crystal 30mm balls (Austrian or German) with hole for hanging**
Colors: clear (general deflector) pink (love), red (abundance) $12.95
+ $1.75 p/h

P. **Hematite Ring, highly polished black stone**
wear while shopping for wise buying (Specify ring size between 5-10)..............$3.50

Q. **Hand Carved Stone Bunnies**
Encourages and can bring romance ....(½") $3.50
....(1") $5.25

R. **Hand Carved Stone Pigs for Wealth**
¾" pig $3.50
Peruvian 1" pig with glass eyes $5.25

S. **Cloisonne Metal "Fancy Tail" Sun Fish with a Jump-Ring**
several colors...$3.50
....or 2/$6.00

FIBER OPTIC ITEMS

Made of fiber optic material which appears as a satin sheen in a vivid color. Please specify color.

Fiber Optic 40mm SPHERES (has a cat's eye appearance)
To deflect ill will and/or to strengthen a gua. (Colors: white, pink, cobalt blue,
yellow, gray, green, teal, black, or purple, instructions included)........................$9.75
+ $2.25 p/h

Fiber Optic DRAGON (1½" long; green, cobalt blue, or teal). $12.00
+ $1.50 p/h

Fiber Optic TIGER (1½" long; white, lavender, or blue). $12.00
+ $1.50 p/h

Fiber Optic PIG or TURTLE (1½" long; white or green)....................................$10.50
+ $1.50 p/h

Fiber Optic RABBIT (1¼" long; white or blue).. $1.50
+ $1.50 p/h

GLASS ITEMS

T. **Two Glass Tan Flutes on Iridescent Blue Oval Leaded Stained Glass** (6" h x 9" w)
Hang in windows, on beams or over doorways. Handmade in U.S.A............... $36.00
+ $3.95 p/h

U. **Ba-Gua Leaded Glass (Window Hanger) Multi-Colored**
Faceted crystal in center on chain. Put on window for balances. $20.00
+ $3.95 p/h

V. **Mirror** (beveled 8" x 8" ba-gua shape) for wall or table
Stimulates positive chi and deflects negative chi/energy...................................$12.95
+ $4.75 p/h

W. **Votive Candle Holder** (Amber glass with gold tone Buddha ornament or
red yin-yang etching) *Please specify color*..$4.95
+ $4.75 p/h

X. **Glass Incense Holder** (10½" long x 1¼" wide)
(Dragon ornament on iridescent blue-purple color and dragonfly on red or Turtle on purple and dolphin on aqua) Incense or essential oils also can be used. *Please specify color* $9.00
+ $2.50 p/h

OILS

Postage & handling for oils: Add $1.50 for 1 bottle; $1.90 for 2 bottles; $2.20 for 3 bottles; and $.25 for each additional.

Abundance (An oil blend to attract prosperity and financial opportunities)
Used by many ancient successful leaders $5.00

Black Pepper (Single oil to remove negative spirits and to use when someone has bad luck)
Can be used in place of Realgar for "Sealing the Door Ceremony"
or for clearing out stagnant energy $5.50

Dream Catcher (An oil blend that enhances mental creativity and daydreams)
Assists in restful sleep and quiets worries..$5.75

Geranium (Single oil to up-lifts moods and help release negative memories)
Brings in fresh energy..$4.00

Harmony (A blend of delicate flower aromas)
Opens meridian center and reduces stress and anxiety.
Has been used in overcoming negative emotions and balances the aura $6.75

Joy (An oil blend for self love and happiness)
Use in S.W. gua or put on your heart. Improves ones self image. Opens you to
accept love and brings more confidence. May be used as an allergy-free perfume...................$5.00

Lavender (A single oil; the universal healing oil, it can soothe stress and is relaxing)
Use in the Tai Chi (center) gua..$3.00

Peace & Calming (An oil blend that relaxes overly active children & helps reduce insomnia)
Brings tranquility to the home...$3.50

Purification (An oil blend that purifies air by removing pollutants, odors, and smoke)
Neutralizes mildew, mold, fungus, and repels mice and insects.
Spray over head or area. Use in all guas $3.00

Release (An oil blend that releases guilt and anxiety)
Is helpful in releasing some traumas, bringing peace and hope. $3.50

White Angelica (An oil blend for spiritual protection)
Removes negative thoughts, protects home from wandering spirits $7.00

For further information about these oils or other oils, please contact us.

To order items:
Send check, money order, or MC/VISA no. & expiration date to:
New Age Concepts, 94 Lark Lane, Bailey CO 80421 • (303) 838-8446 • (303) 838-2282.

Revised March 1999. Prices and availability subject to change without notice.
We often get new and unique items. We welcome inquiries regarding new items,
quantity/wholesale prices, workshops, home, business and land consultations.

COINS

'AMILY FIVE GENERATIONS, COIN

(G) SPIRIT PROTECTION, COIN

HAPPINESS & LONGEVITY, COIN

(D) BUSINESS GOOD LUCK & CONQUERING OBSTACLES, COIN

KILL THE DEVIL" COIN (L)
(K) QUAN-YIN, "GODDESS OF COMPASSION" COIN (R)

(H) YIN-YANG, EXTRA LARGE COIN

(H) YIN-YANG, SMALL COIN

RST ROW

- HEART SHAPED WITH BAMBOO FIGURE, CHARM
- GOOD LUCK IN BUSINESS, ROUND OR HEART SHAPE CHARM
- LONGEVITY & PEACEFUL TRANQUILITY, CHARM

AST ROW

- GOOD LUCK IN BUSINESS, ROUND OR HEART SHAPE CHARM
- SPIRIT PROTECTION, CHARM
- GAMBLING & PROSPERITY, CHARM
- "DOUBLE HAPPINESS" HEART SHAPE CHARM

(X) GLASS INCENSE HOLDER,

Photo of Elaine Jay and Professor Lin 1991.

Elaine Jay Finster is a researcher, public speaker, workshop facilitator, and author. Her most recent books are ABC's of CRYSTALS, and CRYSTALS, GEMS AND RADIONICS. She was the editor and publisher of CRYSTAL PATHWAYS magazine from 1988-90.

A nurse for over 25 years, Elaine Jay left traditional nursing in 1982 to seek alternative healing modalities through holistic concepts. She returned to nursing in 1991 on a part time basis to utilize her holistic approaches along with the allopathic. Crystals, color, and sound have been her main focus. In 1988, she set out on a new path through the means and employment of Feng Shui. After many years of study, practice, and research she began lecturing on this subject little known to westerners. In 1994 she completed her courses in architecture drafting and blueprint reading. Elaine Jay continues to study interior design. She feels that this is a way to blend the ancient east with the modern west.

She travels widely lecturing, teaching classes and doing personal Feng Shui inspection of homes, offices and businesses. Her main focus is readjusting existing homes, businesses, factory adjustments, and ideal land selection.

She studied with Professor Lin Yun of Berkeley, California, the world acclaimed Feng Shui master of the Black Hat Tantric School of Feng Shui.

Elaine Jay and husband Stanley Bytnar both practice the Black Hat style of interior design and placement of Feng Shui. Elaine can be reached at her home office in Bailey, Colorado, (303) 838-8446, 24 Hour FAX (303) 838-2282.